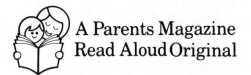

The Giggle Book

Favorite Riddles

selected by Stephanie Calmenson
pictures by Maxie Chambliss

Parents Magazine Press • New York

To Jaime and Erica Stechel—S.C.

To giggling Nicky Fehlinger—M.C.

Library of Congress Cataloging-in-Publication Data
The Giggle book.
Summary: An illustrated collection of riddles, such as
"What did the mayonnaise say to the refrigerator? Close
the door, I'm dressing!"
1. Riddles, Juvenile. [1. Riddles] I. Calmenson,
Stephanie. II. Chambliss, Maxie, ill.
PN6371.5.G48 1987   398'.6   87-9085
ISBN 0-8193-1140-5

Close the door, I'm dressing!

What is smarter than a talking horse?

A spelling bee.

What do you call a carton
full of ducks?

A box of quackers.

What does a polite mouse
always say?

Cheese and thank-you.

What did the judge say when
the skunk walked into court?

Odor in the court!

What did the boy octopus say
to the girl octopus?

I want to hold your hand, hand, hand,
hand, hand, hand, hand, hand.

Who is beautiful, gray
and wears glass slippers?

Cinderelephant.

A squawkestra.

How do you know oysters are lazy?

They are always in their beds.

What has teeth, but never eats?

A comb.

How do you make a hot dog stand?

Take away its chair.

What do hippopotamuses have
that no other animals have?

Baby hippopotamuses.

Why are fish so smart?

Because they live in schools.

How does a witch tell time?

By her witch-watch, of course.

What do you get when an elephant bumps into a cherry tree?

A cherry shake.

What is worse than a centipede
with tired feet?

A giraffe with a sore throat.

Where do cows like to go
on Saturday night?

To the moo-vies.

What day of the week did Noah
march the animals into the ark?

Twos-day.

How did the snake end his letter?

Love and hisses!

About the Author and Artist

Stephanie Calmenson takes giggling very seriously. "I try to giggle at least three times a day," she says. "That means twenty-one giggles a week, which comes to almost one hundred giggles a month, or twelve hundred giggles a year. And if I live to be one hundred (which is possible because giggling is good for you), my lifetime total will be over one hundred thousand."

Maxie Chambliss says, "That's a lot of giggles! I like to giggle too, but if I giggle when I work, my brush jiggles and the paint goes outside the lines. So I let my drawings giggle for me. I've done lots of giggling alligators, a few snickering elephants, and *hundreds* of laughing penguins!"

Stephanie Calmenson and Maxie Chambliss have worked together on six books, including TEN FURRY MONSTERS for Parents. They look forward to working together on many more books in the future.